WHEN THE UNIVERSE WHISPERED HUSH

Text Copyright © 2021 Cristina Cozzone

Illustration rights owned by Cristina Cozzone

Illustrations created by Ugur Kose

Edited by Marjah Simon-Meinefeld

Author Writer's Academy (AWA)

www.AWA4Life.com

ISBN: 9798734054574 Paperback

First Edition

This book belongs to

...........................................................

I used to live in a world
that rushed.

Then the Universe
whispered HUSH!

HUSH

The cities were asked

to listen

until the sun would glisten.

So the world went to sleep.

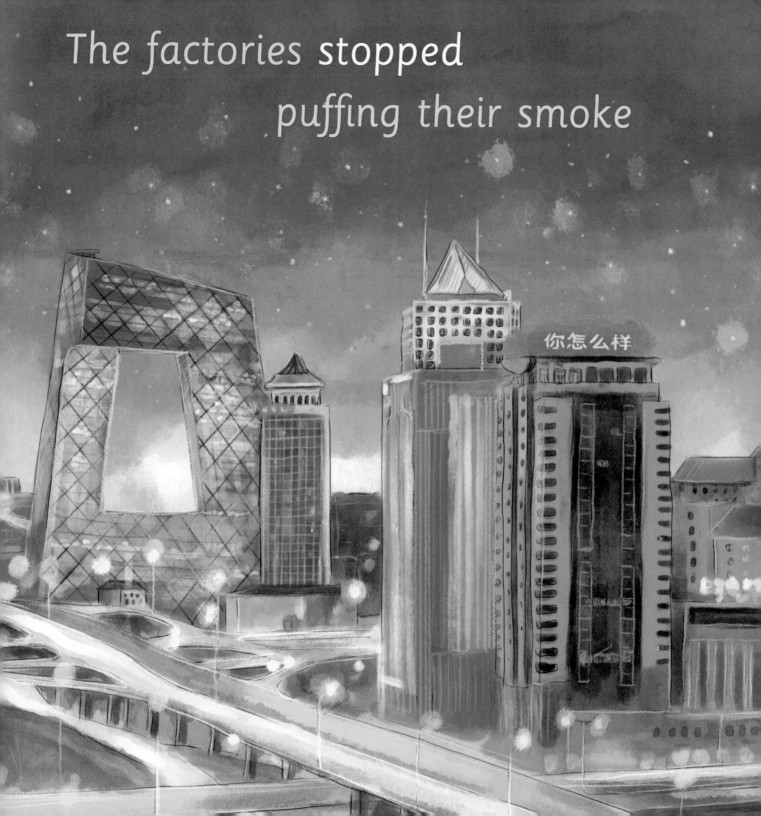

The factories stopped
puffing their smoke

and the boats stopped
chugging to row.

# The Statue of Liberty sat down to read

as noisy horns no longer went beep!

The Universe smiled at the world, for the air was cleaner

and the animals were happy again.

I used to live in a world
that rushed

**HUSH**

before the Universe
whispered HUSH!

Now my family sits
together at dinner

and I feel a whole lot better!

# We share stories and

laugh while playing.

# These are the memories

I love creating.

I am finding happiness
in my home!

I guess the Universe
must have known.

We used to live in a world
that rushed.

Can you hear the Universe
whispering hush?

The following pages are provided for daytime discussions.
When reading this book at night, please stop here.

Dear Readers,

I wrote this book about when the Universe whispered hush! At this time many people were struggling to understand their emotions. You may have also found it challenging to adjust to the changes made. If we choose to only remember the masks, social distancing and missed events, it may leave us feeling sad or frustrated. What would it feel like to also remember the moments of goodness?

In the story, you read about children all over the world, choosing to focus on their happy moments such as spending more time with their families and playing outdoors. They also witnessed people coming together to care for each other and the Earth having time to heal!

This book is about looking for the good even when it may seem impossible. Can you think of three things you are grateful for at this very moment?

I am extremely grateful for you!

Cristina

**Follow-up Questions:**

What do you think this book is about?

Do you remember when you found out about "the Universe whispering hush"?

How did you feel? Happy? Scared? Confused? Loved?

How do you feel today?

Are there things you would like to change?

What would you like to stay the same?

What are you grateful for right now?

**Can You Find These Cities and Fun Facts:**

London, England. Do you see the big clock tower? It is called Big Ben.

Giza, Egypt. The Great Sphinx of Giza is taking a nap- shhh...

Beijing, China. When the factories stopped puffing their smoke, China's air became cleaner. The Chinese characters, on the building, say "How are you?" Characters are similar to words.

Venice, Italy. When the boats stopped chugging to row, the Venice canals became so clear that dolphins and swans came by to visit.

New York, New York. What book do you think the Statue of Liberty is reading?

**Going Deeper:**

Taking care of our emotional health (our feelings) is just as important as taking care of our physical health (our bodies). It is good to know that our feelings often need the same things our bodies do to stay healthy such as good rest and healthy food. Sometimes feelings can take over and we aren't really sure where they came from- adults feel this too! This is when we can go to a menu of options that will help us understand our emotions better.

⭐ We can ask for what we need. A simple hug can make a big difference!

⭐ We can also ask for space. We may need to be alone to feel our feelings.

⭐ We can take deep breaths. Try blowing up a pretend balloon and letting it go slowly, count to 10 or count down from 5.

⭐ We can exercise or get outside. Sometimes our bodies need to release our emotions physically. Try jumping, running, yoga poses or doing a silly dance to your favorite music.

⭐ We can squeeze or hit a pillow. Sometimes our bodies build up so much energy we feel like exploding. Still it is never okay to take this energy out on other people, animals, or objects. Using a pillow makes sure you and others are safe!

⭐ We can get still. Just like when the Universe whispered hush! Can you hear it? Take a moment to be quiet and just listen, try meditation or tapping.

**The Big Picture:**

It is okay to feel all sorts of emotions. In time you will better understand your feelings and what steps you can take to help yourself. Your way may be completely different than a family member or friend's way and that's okay too. Remember each day is a new day!

**An Idea for Parents and Teachers - Cozy Corners:**

I found creating a "Cozy Corner" in my classrooms to be helpful. I have also helped many families create them in their homes. To set up a "Cozy Corner" pick a quiet space. Start with something soft to sit on such as a bean bag chair, a pile of cozy pillows, or a little couch/chair. I often like to put a basket or shelf filled with books nearby. Sensory jars, stress balls and stuffed animals can be a soothing addition. Remember to keep it simple and inviting. The children can help create their space!

When a child is experiencing some feelings and you think they need space to "just be", gently remind them that this may be a good time to just sit with their feelings. Remember this is not meant to be a "time-out" space. Let them decide when they need a break and when they are ready to come back. You can say something like "come join us when you're ready" or "we will be so happy to play again when you come back".

Cristina Cozzone has been working with children ever since she started baby-sitting at nine years old. She has professionally been working with children and their families for over 10 years as a nanny, pre-k teacher and strategic intervention coach. She deeply believes in empowering children and that every child deserves to be loved, cared for, and taught in the way that meets their own personal needs.

Also, at age nine, Cristina was diagnosed with Leukemia and needed a bone marrow transplant. This made her extremely sick so she spent a lot of time in the hospital. After going through her experience, she felt it was important for kids, similar to herself, to have a book that explained what it was like to have cancer. Her very first children's book, Me and My Marrow, was published in 1999 in multiple languages including Spanish and Japanese. It won the Health Information Award for Best Patient Education Book and the American Medical Writers Award for Patient Information in 2000.

Cristina now lives with her husband Brian in Northbrook, Illinois, USA. Cristina is excited to share more empowering books with children around the world!